THE COMMONWEALTH GAMES

MOIRA BUTTERFIELD

W

FRANKLIN WATTS

LONDON • SYDNEY

First published in 2014 by
Franklin Watts
338 Euston Road
London NW1 3BH

Franklin Watts Australia
Level 17/207 Kent Street
Sydney NSW 2000

Editor: Sarah Ridley
Editor in chief: John C. Miles
Design: Graham Rich Design
Art director: Peter Scoulding
Picture research: Diana Morris

A CIP catalogue record for this book
is available from the British Library.

Dewey Decimal Classification Number: 796'.091712'41

ISBN (hardback): 978 1 4451 2783 5
ISBN (library ebook): 978 1 4451 2784 2

Printed in China

Franklin Watts is a division of Hachette Children's Books,
an Hachette UK company.

www.hachette.co.uk

Picture credits

Daniel Berehulak/Getty Images: 15, 26c. Michael Bradley/ Getty Images: 17. Cancan Chu/Getty Images: 14b. Phil Cole/Getty Images: 13. Commonwealth Secretariat: 5t. This map is reproduced from/based upon Ordnance Survey material with permission of Ordnance Survey on behalf of the Controller of Her Majesty's Stationery Office, © Crown Copyright: 20c. Mark Dadswell/Getty Images: front cover l, back cover, 6t, 7, 8, 9t. Lucas Dawson/Getty Images: 27. Empics//PAI: 28-29. Laurent Fieret/Getty Images: 12t. Fox Photos/Hulton Archive/Getty Images: 4b. Stuart Hannagan/Getty Images: 11b. Hulton Archive /Getty Images: 4t. Matt King/Getty Images: front cover c, 16. Mark Kolbe/Getty Images: front cover r, 1, 19, 21t, 21b. Chris McGrath/Getty Images: 20t. Suzanne Plunkett/WPA/ Getty Images: 5c. Adam Pretty/Getty Images: 10b. Ryan Remiorz/Canadian Press/PAI: 11tr. Cameron Spencer/ Getty Images: 11t, 17t. 23. Michael Steele/Getty Images: 6b. Tumar/Shutterstock: 26t. Lilyana Vynogradova/ Shutterstock: 24, 25b. Phil Walter/Getty Images: 18. Ian Walton/Getty Images: 14t, 25t. Michael Weber/Superstock: 9c. William West/AFP/Getty Images: 22.

Every attempt has been made to clear copyright. Should there be any inadvertent omission, please apply to the publisher for rectification.

The statistics contained in this book were correct at the time of printing, but because of the nature of sport, it cannot be guaranteed that they are now accurate.

Note to parents and teachers

Every effort has been made by the Publishers to ensure that the web sites in this book are suitable for children, that they are of the highest educational value, and that they contain no inappropriate or offensive material. However, because of the nature of the Internet, it is impossible to guarantee that the contents of these sites will not be altered. We strongly advise that Internet access is supervised by a responsible adult.

CONTENTS

THE COMMONWEALTH COMES TOGETHER

Every four years, 53 of the world's nations send their best sportspeople to compete in the Commonwealth Games, one of the biggest sports events in the world.

For the first few years, the Commonwealth Games were known as the British Empire Games.

South African Louis Fouche prepares to release the shot put to win gold at the 1938 British Empire Games.

What is the Commonwealth?

The Commonwealth is a group of 53 nations, most of which were once part of the British Empire. Although these countries are now independent, they come together to support each other and work towards shared goals. There are around two billion people living in the Commonwealth, a quarter of the world's population. Their representatives meet together regularly, and every four years their teams compete in the Games. You can find the complete list of Commonwealth member countries online (see page 31).

The growing Games

In 1930, when the Games began, only 11 teams competed in Hamilton, Canada. Today, over 70 teams take part in the Commonwealth Games. They include the Commonwealth nations, British territories overseas and the home nations of England, Scotland, Wales and Northern Ireland in separate teams. In 1930 there were 59 events in six sports. Today there are more than 250 events in many different sports! They include events found in the Olympic Games but also sports played mainly in Commonwealth countries, such as lawn bowls, rugby sevens and netball. There are now para-sport events at the Games, too.

COMMONWEALTH QUICK FACTS

The Games are the world's third-biggest sports event, after the Olympic Games and the Asian Games.

In the year before the Games begin, the Games' baton is taken on a 190,000-km journey around the Commonwealth.

The official flag of the Commonwealth. Look out for it when you watch the Games.

The Queen of the Games

The British monarch, Queen Elizabeth II, is currently the Head of the Commonwealth. Before each Games, a message from the Queen is placed inside a specially designed baton. It is carried in a relay around all the Commonwealth countries, touching down in Asia, Oceania, North and South America, the Caribbean and Europe before it arrives at the opening ceremony. There the message is finally taken from the baton and read out to the crowd.

For the 2010 Games held in Delhi, India, the Queen's baton contained a message of support for the Commonwealth written on gold leaf inside a jewelled box. The baton was also fitted with a video camera, microphone, LED lighting and a GPS tracking system.

TEARING UP THE TRACK

Olympic champions compete alongside new young track stars for Commonwealth glory on the athletics track. The events range from super-fast sprinting to middle- and long-distance running events, a marathon and para-sport track contests.

Natasha Mayers of St Vincent and the Grenadines (dark green kit) wins gold in the 100m in 2010.

Superfast sprinting

The 100m, 200m and 400m races are known as the sprints. The runners explode into action from blocks fitted with sensors which register a false start, (if someone starts too soon). The competitors stay in eight numbered lanes and the winner is the first athlete to get his or her torso (upper body) over the line. The Commonwealth's Caribbean runners are the world's most successful sprinting stars. Their men's 100m specialists consistently run under 10 seconds, making them the fastest humans on the planet.

Runners bunch together towards the end of a middle-distance race. Scotland's Stephanie Twell is in the foreground.

In it for the long run

The 800m and 1,500m races are known as the middle-distance events, whereas the 5,000m and 10,000m races are known as the long-distance competitions. In both categories, the runners start in staggered lanes and eventually bunch together in one inside lane, pounding round and around the track. The athletes must try to conserve their energy, stay in a good position, and get ready to sprint when the finish line is in sight. The 10,000m can take half an hour or more to run, so the athletes need fantastic stamina.

Superfast superstars
Here are some of the greatest Commonwealth track results:

MEN'S EVENTS
100m — 9.88 secs — Ato Boldon, Trinidad and Tobago, 1998
200m — 19.97 secs — Frankie Fredericks, Namibia, 1994
400m — 44.52 secs — Iwan Thomas, Wales, 1998
800m — 1.43.22 — Steve Cram, England, 1986

WOMEN'S EVENTS
100m — 10.91 secs — Debbie Ferguson, Bahamas, 2002
200m — 22.19 secs — Merlene Ottey, Jamaica, 1982
400m — 50.10 secs — Amantle Montsho, Botswana, 2010
800m — 1.57.35 — Maria Mutola, Mozambique, 2002

Ram Singh Yadav of India (left) and Jeffrey Hunt of Australia compete in the men's marathon in New Delhi, 2010.

Medal-winning marathon

The Commonwealth's African athletes are often the marathon superstars, especially Kenya's world-beating long-distance runners. The marathon starts and finishes at the host city's main athletics arena, such as Glasgow's Hampden Park. It is run through the streets of the city, past its most famous landmarks, with crowds lining the route. The official marathon distance is 42.195km, which is the same for every marathon run around the world. The men usually complete their event in just over 2 hours and the women take around 2 hours and 25 minutes.

COMMONWEALTH QUICK FACTS

All athletics events are run anti-clockwise, but nobody is sure why.

During the first Games in 1930, the competitors slept in the classrooms of a local school.

GO HIGH, GO LONG

In the centre of the athletics stadium the Commonwealth athletes take part in the jumping and throwing competitions known as field events.

Soaring high

The high jump, long jump, triple jump and pole vault events provide tough tests for the athletes and exciting contests for the spectators. The high jumpers and pole vaulters must clear a bar that gets gradually higher during the competition, but if they knock the bar down three times at the same height, they are eliminated. Long jumpers and triple jumpers sprint along a runway and launch themselves into a sandpit, but if their foot lands in front of a board as they take off, the jump does not count. The triple jumpers have to make tricky hop and step movements before they jump.

Jamaican athlete Trecia-Kaye Smith competes in the triple jump competition in 2010, where she won gold.

COMMONWEALTH QUICK FACTS

The long jump was an ancient Greek sport. It may have been invented to simulate jumping over streams and ravines.

Equipment for throwing sports (such as the javelin and discus) is heavier for men than it is for women.

Hammer-throwing developed as a sport in Scotland, where it has long been part of the Highland Games.

Throwing Long

The discus, javelin, shot put and hammer-throwing events are based on some of the oldest sports in the world. The ancient Greeks threw the javelin and the discus in competitions. Their soldiers threw javelins in battle, and they prized sports that displayed a warrior's skills. All the throwing sports have a marked-out throwing area, and athletes must stay within the markings until their throw has landed. A net around the area prevents the equipment accidently flying backwards and hurting onlookers.

Canadian hammer thrower Megann Rodhe competes in the 2010 Games.

A judge shows a red flag if a jump breaks the rules.

Tough technique

Doing well in field sports depends on athletes learning careful techniques. The jumpers must get their stride patterns right as they run and make sure their body is at the right angle for a jump. The throwers must get their footwork right, as well as their arm movement. Unusual ways of throwing and jumping are not allowed and there are strict rules on the size, shape and weight of equipment. Judges stand alongside each event, checking on technique and confirming the results of each competitor.

Fantastic in the field

Here are some of the greatest Commonwealth jumps and throws:

MEN'S EVENTS

Pole vault — 5.8m — Steven Hooker, Australia, 2006
High jump — 2.36m — Clarence Saunders, Bermuda, 1990
Long jump — 8.39m — Yusuf Alli, Nigeria, 1990
Javelin — 89.48m — Mike O'Rourke, New Zealand, 1982
Discus — 66.39m — Frantz Kruger, South Africa, 2002

WOMEN'S EVENTS

Pole vault — 4.62m — Kym Howe, Australia, 2006
High jump — 1.96m — Hestrie Cloete, South Africa, 2002
Long jump — 6.97m — Bronwyn Thompson, Australia, 2006
Javelin — 69.8m — Tessa Sanderson, England, 1986
Discus — 65.92m — Beatrice Faumuina, New Zealand, 1998

WINNING IN WATER

Some of the world's top swimmers can be seen powering through the pool at the Commonwealth Games, while divers amaze the crowd by taking breathtaking plunges. There are para-swimming medals to be won, too.

COMMONWEALTH QUICK FACTS

Synchronised swimming is an optional Commonwealth sport. It was not picked for inclusion in the 2014 Games.

Australia heads the all-time Commonwealth swimming medal table by a long way. Canada and England are next in the table.

There is no age-limit to competing in the Commonwealth pool. Over the years several swimming and diving gold medallists have won at the age of only 13 or 14.

Speedy swimming

Fractions of a second separate the swimmers in the 50m-long Commonwealth pool. They swim in eight lanes over varying lengths, using different swimming techniques, depending on their event. Spectators get to see breaststroke, butterfly, backstroke and freestyle (crawl), the fastest of the swimming strokes. All the swimmers must qualify through heats before they reach the finals, so they need strength and stamina to swim more than once.

Australian Commonwealth Games superstar Leisel Jones.

At the end of each lane there is an electronic pad that records the touch of a swimmer's fingertips.

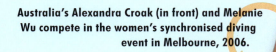

Australia's Alexandra Croak (in front) and Melanie Wu compete in the women's synchronised diving event in Melbourne, 2006.

Para-swimming events are a big part of the Commonwealth Games.

Pool perfection

There are 1m, 3m and 10m diving boards, and events for both individual divers and synchronised teams, whose every movement must be perfectly co-ordinated to get top marks. A dive may be over in seconds but it will have taken many hours of practice! Judges score the competitors on their dive approach, their take-off, their plunge and their landing. They must enter the water with their bodies as close to a vertical (straight) position as possible, or they lose marks. Medal-winning scores are usually around 8.5 to 9.5.

The stars from Down Under

Australia's world-beating swimming stars usually rule the pool at the Commonwealth Games. Ian Thorpe, nicknamed the Thorpedo, won four golds in 1998 and a further six in 2002. Susie O'Neill gathered an amazing 15 medals, ten of them gold, in three Games – 1990, 1994 and 1998. But Ian and Susie's gold hauls can't top Aussie women's golden girl Leisel Jones, who won 11 gold medals in three Games – 2002, 2006 and 2010.

Australia's Ian Thorpe wins gold in 2002.

DOING IT ALL

Commonwealth triathletes need to be able to swim, cycle and run, and be outstanding at all three to get a shot at a medal.

Lucky number 3

A triathlon has three gruelling stages. The triathletes start with a 1,500m swim in open water (outdoors), then hop on a bicycle for a 40km cycle race, followed by a 10km run. In between each section there are timed 'transition' stages, when the athletes must quickly change their clothing ready for the next challenge. They need to be able to pace themselves through the whole event and have enough power left for a strong final run.

Triathlon competitors dive in to begin the gruelling three-sport test of speed and endurance.

COMMONWEALTH QUICK FACTS

The word 'triathlon' is made up of two ancient Greek words – meaning a 'contest of three'.

The triathletes wear electronic timing bands to record their progress as they swim, cycle and run.

Superfast and super fun

There is a fast-moving and exciting new Commonwealth event – a mixed triathlon relay with two men and two women in each team. The team members take it in turns to complete a shortened 'super sprint' triathlon – a 400m swim, a 10km cycle race and a 2.5km run. They must then tag the next member of their team, who begins their own short triathlon.

Triathlon stages

Here are the stages in a triathlon event:

1. When the gun goes, the athletes race to the water, wearing wetsuits, swimming caps and goggles. They must quickly try to get to the front, so they can swim forward into clear water. In the crowded water behind it's not so easy, as there can be lots of accidental elbowing and kicking.

2. At the transition stage the triathletes must pull off their swimming kit (they wear a singlet underneath). They must put on a cycling helmet and grab their bike, which will have their cycling shoes already clipped to the pedals, to save time.

3. After the ride they must slip on their running shoes (with pre-tied elastic laces) and get going on the final run.

Canadian Carol Montgomery wins the women's triathlon in 2002.

Commonwealth triathlon records

Men's individual triathlon: 1 hr, 49 mins, 16 secs — Bradley Kahlefeldt, Australia, 2006

Women's individual triathlon: 1 hr, 58 mins, 2 secs — Emma Snowsill, Australia, 2006

GOLDEN RACKETS

The Commonwealth's top squash, badminton and table tennis players take part in lightning-quick contests, hoping to qualify for a medal match.

Fast and feathery

Badminton is said to be the fastest racket sport in the world, and the players need great anticipation skills to reach shuttlecocks that zoom across the net at more than 300kph. They need to be able to lunge, leap and stretch, too. England and Malaysia have been the top badminton nations for a while, but India, Scotland and Singapore are rising stars.

The Indian women's doubles team play speedy badminton in the 2010 Games.

Glass walls allow spectators to see squash matches from all angles. This picture shows David Palmer of Australia (right) and Peter Nicol of England in the men's squash final in Melbourne, 2006.

Small ball. big game

Squash players must be super-fit to move around the court quickly, but they must also be able to hit the ball at just the right angle. Squash is played with small bouncy rubber balls, and in top competitions players use balls which are less bouncy than those used in ordinary games, making them harder to play. Australia and England are very successful at this level, but Malaysia, New Zealand, India and Pakistan are also contenders. The medal matches take place in a show court that looks like a big glass box, with four toughened see-through walls.

COMMONWEALTH
QUICK FACTS

Shuttlecocks are made of goose feathers, always taken from the left wing. The left-hand feathers curve in a way that makes the shuttlecock aerodynamic.

Squash has been played since the 1800s. There was a squash court on the *Titanic,* in the first class section of the ship.

Table tennis was invented by British military officers, who played on dinner tables using champagne corks as balls and box lids as bats.

Watch that spin

Table tennis players need split-second reactions because the ball can shoot across the net at up to 113kph in a top-level competition match. Top players are experts at spinning the ball, hitting it at an angle to make it change direction in unexpected ways. Singapore is the top Commonwealth table tennis medal-winning country, followed by Australia, England and India.

Singapore table tennis ace Mengyu Yu concentrates hard on the ball as she begins to serve.

FIGHT TO WIN

The Commonwealth combat sports – freestyle wrestling, judo and boxing – are contested by bouts between two opponents, with the winner going through to another round and perhaps eventually to a medal contest.

COMMONWEALTH QUICK FACTS

Unlike professional boxers, all amateur boxers wear headguards. The boxers at the Commonwealth Games are all amateurs.

The freestyle wrestlers wear singlets made of slippery nylon or lycra, making them hard to grab and hold in a bout.

Wrestling is one of the oldest organised sports in the world. It was a popular sport in ancient Greece.

A knockout sport

Boxing is organised by weight, so people of the same size and build fight each other. Boxers win by either knocking out an opponent or getting the best score from the boxing judges watching the fight. The judges count up the number of clean blows landed on target during the three or four rounds of the contest. Canada and the UK nations are strong Commonwealth contenders but the African nations have lots of young talent. From 2014, women boxers can take part in the Commonwealth Games, too.

Tariq Abdul Haqq of Trinidad and Tobago (left) competes against Paramjeet Samota of India in the over 91 kg men's boxing finals in New Delhi, 2010.

Grappling for gold

Men and women have their own freestyle wrestling competitions. Wrestlers can win by a 'fall' – forcing their opponent's shoulders onto the mat – or by gaining the highest technical score from the judges at the end of a bout. Judges award points for skilful moves such as holds and throws.

Wrestling relies on strength but also on controlling an opponent's moves, so competitors have to stay very focused.

Combat judo-style

If you were wearing a *judogi* and trying to score an *ippon* you would be taking part in judo. The judogi is the loose-fitting outfit worn for bouts, and an ippon is the winning move of throwing an opponent on their back. Contestants use armholds and body locks to score points, or they can win rounds outright with an ippon. UK nations, Australia and Canada are usually strong contenders.

Women judo competitors wear loose-fitting judogi outfits. Here, Elinor Stalworthy from New Zealand (in white) competes with Sisilia Nagisa of Fiji in Manchester, 2002.

WE DO THIS TOGETHER

Team players must rely on each other, working together to get their tactics right in the hockey, netball and rugby sevens events.

Shoot for glory

Twelve women's netball teams compete for one precious Commonwealth gold medal. The Commonwealth nations field the world's best netball teams, so the action is fast-paced, with quick, exciting shifts between defence and attack. Each player has a specific position which limits where they can go on the court, and they wear bibs showing their position initials. For instance, only two positions – goal attack (GA) and goal shooter (GS) – can shoot for goal. Australia and New Zealand are regular Commonwealth finalists but England, Jamaica, South Africa and Malawi are all possible contenders, too.

Jamaica plays England in the 2010 netball contest.

COMMONWEALTH QUICK FACTS

It's estimated that netball is played by more than 20 million people in around 80 countries around the world.

Hockey is the national sport of Pakistan, who always send strong teams to the Games.

In countries where ice hockey is played, ordinary hockey is called 'field hockey'.

Fourteen-minute medal

Men's rugby sevens is hard to beat for fast and furious team action, with plenty of points scored. Sixteen rugby sevens teams compete for only one gold medal, so there is all to play for in the fourteen-minute matches. A normal rugby team has 15 players, but a sevens team has only three forwards and four backs. They run around on a full-sized pitch, so they have to be fit!

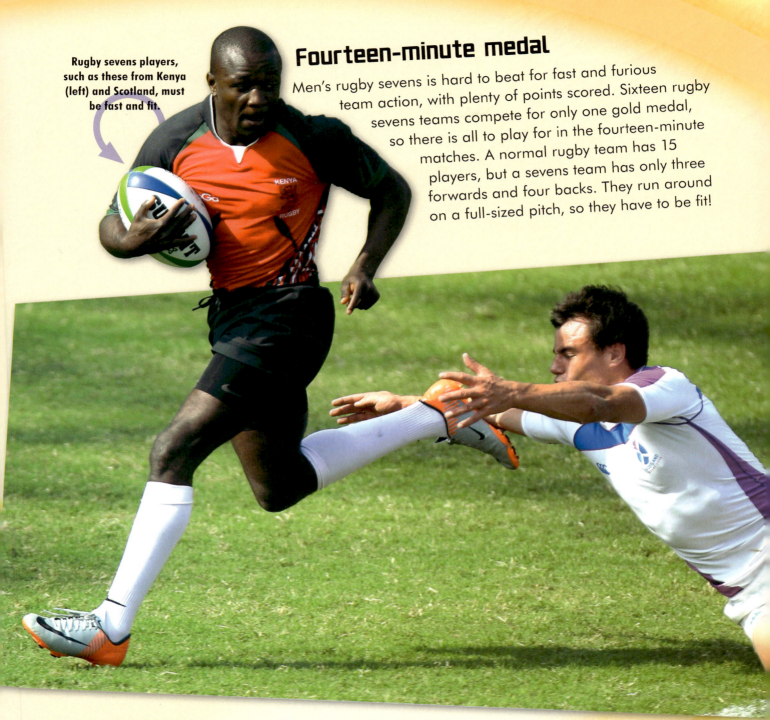

Rugby sevens players, such as these from Kenya (left) and Scotland, must be fast and fit.

Twenty teams, two golds

In men's and women's hockey, each team goes into a pool (a group of teams that play each other), and the pool winners contest the medal positions. If teams draw there are nail-biting extra-time sessions, with golden goals (instant winning goals) or tense penalty shoot-outs. Australia's teams are the Commonwealth kings and queens of hockey, with lots of gold medals in their collection, but they often face strong teams from Pakistan, England, India, New Zealand and Malaysia.

WINNING ON WHEELS

The Commonwealth's best cyclists compete for mountain bike racing, road racing and track racing medals. Commonwealth countries provide some of the world's top talent, so the contests are very competitive and exciting to watch.

A bumpy ride

Mountain bikers need to be able to ride as fast as possible over rocks and streams, up steep hills, round tight corners and down steps. Their bikes are rugged and strong, and designed to make the ride feel less bumpy for the cyclist onboard. Courses are designed to test all the bikers' skills, and individual course features are given names. Here is a run-through of the 2014 Commonwealth Games mountain biking course. Its features were named by Scottish schoolchildren.

2014 MOUNTAIN BIKE COURSE

Propeller Point – A maze of rocks where riders can overtake each other, by picking a different line (route) through the rocks.

Double Dare – A double trail down an open hillside. Riders can choose either track.

Clyde Climb – A steep rocky hill, which gives the fittest riders an advantage.

Rest and be Thankful – A switchback climb, a plateau and downward track. Riders can choose an easier but slower downward route, or a harder but faster line.

Broken Biscuits – Rocks and drops favour the most technically-skilled riders.

The Jouk – Several banked and curved corners called berms.

Brig o' Doom – Twists and turns up over rocks, a bridge over a stream, a super-tight turn and a water splash.

Boulder Dash – Riders sprint towards the finish over a causeway of bumpy boulders, with steps and drops.

Racing the roads

There are road races and time trials for men and women cyclists held on roads around the Commonwealth host city. The road racers compete in national teams made up of five cyclists with different skills. A team will have good climbers, quick sprinters and time trial specialists who are able to go fast over long distances. They all work together, pacing each other to keep their team leader in a good position, ready to win at the end. In the time trial events, cyclists ride along the course individually, trying to achieve the fastest time.

Road racing bikes are very lightweight and fast. They have lots of gears for different riding conditions, such as steep hills or fast descents.

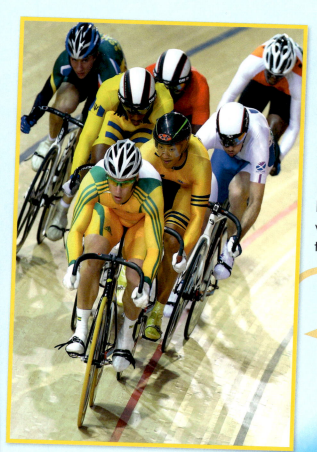

Track cycling – the long and the short

Track cycling takes place in a velodrome, an indoor arena with a banked (sloped) track. Track bikes are designed for riding on a smooth surface. They don't have brakes and they have only one gear. There are fast sprint races and longer-distance endurance races for teams and individuals. The cyclists must be super-fit but very good at tactics, too. They must watch their opponents carefully and make a move to win at just the right time.

Australia won a record 12 gold track cycling medals at the 2010 Games.

COMMONWEALTH QUICK FACTS

The 2014 Glasgow velodrome was named after Scottish track cyclist Sir Chris Hoy. With six gold medals, he is Britain's most successful Olympian.

Tandem cycling was a Commonwealth event in the 1970s.

FANTASTIC GYMNASTICS

Commonwealth gymnasts need strength, flexibility and great balance. Their routines are scored for technique and artistic presentation, and they only stand a chance of a medal if they put in many hours of training!

Two paths to glory

There are two different gymnastics categories in the Games. In artistic gymnastics, competitors use equipment such as the pommel horse, vault, rings, beam and bars, and they also perform routines on an exercise surface called the floor. In rhythmic gymnastics, the performers use handheld apparatus such as hoops, balls, clubs and ribbons to create a smooth skilled performance.

Louis Smith, English Commonwealth gold and bronze medal winner, on the pommel horse.

MELBOURNE 2006

ACROMA

Rhythmic routines

The rhythmic gymnasts perform to music, individually or in teams. Judges give them points for technical moves such as leaps, balances and pirouettes. They also get points for handling their apparatus well, and for the artistic effect of it. They choose their music, their costumes, and the overall style of their performance, and practise their routine for many hours to make it as perfect as possible. If they are performing together as a team, they must be totally synchronised.

Australia's star rhythmic gymnast, Naazmi Johnston, won three golds and two silvers at the 2010 Games.

Strength and artistry

The artistic gymnasts perform in individual events and team events, too. They often train for 30 hours or more each week, honing their technique and fitness, repeating and re-repeating the moves that will score them high points. On the big day, the judges give them points for their technical ability and their artistic interpretation, but knock off points for mistakes such as stumbling. Not only must gymnasts be strong, they must also know how to hold their body in the right position, or the judges could deduct marks. For instance, in the pommel horse event (for men), competitors must walk up and down the pommel horse using their hands, while keeping their legs perfectly straight and together.

HIT THE TARGET

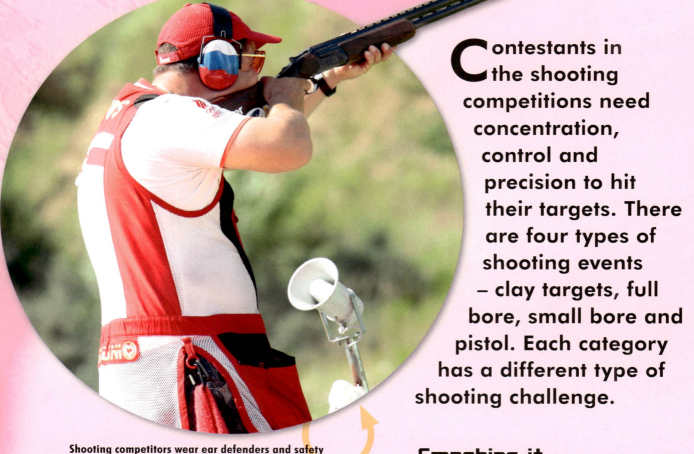

Shooting competitors wear ear defenders and safety glasses to prevent injury as they fire.

Contestants in the shooting competitions need concentration, control and precision to hit their targets. There are four types of shooting events – clay targets, full bore, small bore and pistol. Each category has a different type of shooting challenge.

Smashing it

The clay target shooters face a stream of moving disc-shaped clay targets zooming across their line of vision. They must fire a shotgun with super-fine accuracy to hit and smash as many of the targets as possible, fired from a machine called a trap. The trap can fire single or double clay targets out at different speeds and angles, and a puff of powder signals when a clay is hit and a score is registered. The competitors must have fast reactions, an eagle eye and the ability to stay calm under high pressure. If they are not calm, they are likely to lose their ability to aim!

COMMONWEALTH QUICK FACTS

Lots of different Commonwealth countries win shooting medals. It's a very wide-open competition.

Clay target shooting is sometimes called clay pigeon shooting because live pigeons were once used instead of clay discs.

Competitors lie on the ground in the full bore rifle event.

His 'n hers shooting

The full bore rifle event is unique to the Commonwealth Games and features two competitions – singles and pairs. It's also special because it is one of the few sports in the world where men and women compete against each other in the same contest. They must fire at a number of different targets set apart to a distance of 914m. The closer they get to the middle of each target, the higher they score. They lie on the ground, with their single shot target rifle held in a sling to keep it steady. However, wind can play a big part, blowing their shots off-course, so they must check the flags set up around the course to judge how best to aim.

Computer sensors accurately record a shooter's performance.

Bullseye!

In the small bore and pistol events, the competitors fire at electronic targets marked with ten rings, each one scoring differently. The circle in the very centre of the ring scores highest. They must concentrate and keep calm, firing a certain number of shots in a limited time, depending on the event they have entered. Some competitors lie down, others kneel to shoot at their targets. They must try to block out all thoughts of the audience and the TV cameras trained on them, following their every move!

STRONG CONTENDERS

The weightlifters lift barbells – metal bars loaded with weighted discs. The more discs, the heavier the barbell, which can be more than twice the athlete's own weight.

Heavy barbell discs are loaded on either side of a metal bar.

India's Farman Basha competes in the powerlifting bench para-sports event in 2010.

Lifting lots

There are men's and women's events in different weight categories, and all the lifting is overseen by referees (the competitors must lift properly, or their attempt doesn't count). There are two different lifting techniques. In a 'snatch' lift, an athlete hoists the barbell up above the head in one movement. In a 'clean and jerk' lift, a competitor lifts the barbell to chest height, then jerks it up higher. The competitor must then stand, holding the weights up, until the referee gives a signal.

Perfect para-lifting

Prepare to be impressed and amazed by the strength on show in the Commonwealth para-sport men's and women's weightlifting events. Here the competitors need super-strong arm and stomach muscles to 'bench-press' the barbell – pushing it up from a lying-down position on a bench. Unlike the non-disabled weightlifters, they cannot use the power of their legs to help them lift, so they must rely on their upper body.

COMMONWEALTH QUICK FACTS

Nigeria is a star Commonwealth weightlifting nation.

GOLD ON GRASS

Lawn bowls is a popular Commonwealth sport, and several world champions are from Commonwealth countries. It may look like a relaxed event, but it takes clever strategy, pinpoint precision and concentration to be a success.

How it's done

Competitors must roll their bowls towards a small white ball called a jack. They take turns, trying to get closer to the jack than their opponents and accumulating points during a match. The bowls are not perfectly round; they are shaped so that they follow a curve – a 'bias' – as they roll, and the players must know just how to judge their distance and direction. There are events for singles, doubles, threesomes and foursomes.

Rob Weale of Wales, who has a Games record of six lawn bowls medals.

COMMONWEALTH QUICK FACTS

The world's oldest bowling green is in Southampton, UK. It dates back to 1299.

Winning together

Visually impaired people take part in the Commonwealth para-sport lawn bowls. They are paired with a sighted partner who gives them directions on the direction and strength needed to bowl towards the jack. People with other physical impairments have their own event, and can use specially-designed wheelchairs if they need to.

THE GLASGOW GAMES

On 23 July 2014, a big opening ceremony signals the start of the 20th Commonwealth Games, 11 days of fantastic sporting competition held in and around the Scottish city of Glasgow. It's the largest multi-sport event that Scotland has ever hosted.

Get ready, Glasgow!

In 2010 a billion TV viewers and 60,000 spectators looked on as the official Commonwealth Games flag was handed over to Scotland by India, who staged the Games in Delhi. That night, 348 young Scottish volunteers put on a dance and music show to celebrate Scottish history and send the Games officially on their way to Glasgow. The 2014 Games has its own spectacular opening ceremony at the Celtic Park stadium, and a closing ceremony at the Hampden Park stadium.

Venues at the XX Games 256 medal events, including 22 para-sport medals

Aquatics (inc: para-sport events) – Tollcross International Swimming Centre

Athletics (inc: para-sport events) – Hampden Park

Badminton – SECC (Scottish Exhibition and Conference Centre)

Boxing – SECC (Scottish Exhibition and Conference Centre)

Cycling (inc: para-sport events) – Sir Chris Hoy Velodrome (track cycling), Cathkin Braes Country Park (mountain biking), Glasgow streets (road cycling)

Gymnastics – SECC (Scottish Exhibition and Conference Centre)

Hockey – Glasgow National Hockey Centre

Judo – SECC (Scottish Exhibition and Conference Centre)

Lawn Bowls (inc: para-sport events) – Kelvingrove Lawn Bowls Centre

Netball – SECC (Scottish Exhibition and Conference Centre)

Rugby Sevens – Ibrox Stadium

Shooting – Barry Buddon Shooting Centre

Squash – Scotstoun Sports Campus

Table Tennis – Scotstoun Sports Campus

Triathlon – Strathclyde Country Park

Weightlifting (inc: para-sport events) – SECC (Scottish Exhibition and Conference Centre)

Wrestling – SECC (Scottish Exhibition and Conference Centre)

Sporting spots

The sports take place in venues around Glasgow, in the nearby countryside and in Edinburgh. The Athlete's Village, in Dalmarnock on the banks of the River Clyde, houses 6,000 athletes and officials, and when the Games finish it will be turned into homes for local people. Around 260,000 items from the 2012 London Olympics Village are being re-used in the Commonwealth Village, and the rooms are decorated with art created by schoolchildren all over Scotland.

The Scottish Exhibition and Conference Centre precinct, used for the Commonwealth Games in 2014.

COMMONWEALTH QUICK FACTS

Each sport has its own official symbol, used on signs around the Games.

The motto of the XX Games is 'People, Place, Passion'.

GLOSSARY

Aerodynamic A smooth shape that slips easily through the air.

Artistic gymnastics Gymnastic events using equipment such as the pommel horse, vault, rings, beam bars and floor.

Barbell A metal weightlifting bar loaded with heavy discs on either end.

British Empire The countries ruled to some degree by and from Britain. It reached its greatest extent in the 1920s.

British territories Land abroad that is under British rule.

Clay target A plate-shaped shooting target flung up into the air.

Clean and jerk lift A type of lift when a weightlifter hoists a barbell (bar loaded with weights) to chest height, then jerks it up higher.

Commonwealth A group of 53 nations, most of which were once part of the British Empire.

False start When a race competitor starts too early, before the official start signal.

Field events The jumping and throwing competitions, which take place in the centre of the main athletics stadium.

Freestyle A fast swimming style also known as the crawl.

Golden goal A winning goal in extra time, meaning instant victory.

Head of the Commonwealth The figurehead of the Commonwealth organisation (currently the British monarch, Queen Elizabeth II).

Heats Rounds which competitors must win to progress to medal contests.

Hockey pool A group of hockey teams that play each other, with the pool winners going through to the next round.

Ippon Throwing an opponent on their back, a winning move in judo.

Jack A small white ball used in lawn bowls. Competitors aim bowls towards the jack.

Judogi A loose-fitting outfit worn for judo bouts.

Long distance Races that take place over longer distances. In track athletics, the 5,000m and 10,000m races are known as the long-distance competitions.

Marathon A 42.19km running race over a street course.

Middle distance Races taking place over mid-distances. The 800m and 1,500m athletics track races are known as middle-distance events.

Mountain bike A bicycle designed to cope with bumpy off-road cycling.

Para-sport Sports events for disabled athletes.

Pole vault An event where an athlete runs up to a high bar and tries to sail over it using a pole.

Queen's baton relay A ceremonial baton carried on a route around the Commonwealth countries prior to the opening of the Games.

Rhythmic gymnastics Gymnastics events where performers use handheld apparatus such as hoops, balls, clubs and ribbons.

Shuttlecock A rounded cork shape fitted with goose feathers, used in badminton.

Snatch lift A type of lift when a weightlifter hoists weights up above the head in one movement.

Spin shot When a table tennis player angles his/her bat in contact with the ball, to make it spin as it flies through the air.

Sprints Short fast races. On the athletics track, the 100m, 200m and 400m races are known as the sprints.

Super sprint triathlon A 400m swim, a 10km cycle race and a 2.5km run (all shorter than a full triathlon).

Synchronised diving A diving event, when a team of two dive side-by-side, trying to do exactly the same body movements.

Time triallist A cyclist who specialises in getting the fastest time possible over a road cycling course.

Track bike A bicycle designed for riding on a smooth surface, with no brakes and only one gear.

Transition stages The parts of a triathlon where competitors change their clothing and equipment to do another sport.

Triathlon An event with three sections – swimming, cycling and running.

Triple jump An event where an athlete runs up to a sandpit, takes a hop and a skip, and then tries to jump a long distance.

Velodrome An indoor cycling arena with a banked (sloped) track.

TIMELINE

1930 Hamilton, Canada

1934 London, England

1938 Sydney, Australia

1950 Auckland, New Zealand

1954 Vancouver, Canada

1958 Cardiff, Wales

1962 Perth, Australia

1966 Kingston, Jamaica

1970 Edinburgh, Scotland

1974 Christchurch, New Zealand

1978 Edmonton, Canada

1982 Brisbane, Australia

1986 Edinburgh, Scotland

1990 Auckland, New Zealand

1994 Victoria, Canada

1998 Kuala Lumpur, Malaysia

2002 Manchester, England

2006 Melbourne, Australia

2010 Delhi, India

2014 Glasgow, Scotland

2018 Gold Coast, Australia

WEBLINKS

www.glasgow2104.com The official website of the 2014 Commonwealth Games, where you can see the schedule and find out about the venues.

http://www.thecgf.com The website of the Commonwealth Games Federation, which organises the Games. Find out about the countries taking part and click on the page of your favourite team.

http://www.thecommonwealth.org/ The website of the Commonwealth, with a list of countries involved.

http://www.paralympic.org Paralympic sport around the world.

http://www.weareengland.org The website of the English Commonwealth team.

http://www.teamwales.net/ The website of the Welsh Commonwealth team.

http://www.cgcs.org.uk/team-scotland/about-team-scotland/ The website of the Scottish Commonwealth team.

http://www.nicgc.org/glasgow-2014/team-ni/ The website of the Northern Irish Commonwealth team.

INDEX